Hard Feelings

poems by

Elizabeth R. McCarthy

Finishing Line Press
Georgetown, Kentucky

Hard Feelings

ACKNOWLEDGMENTS

Poetry Society of Vermont—The Mountain Troubadour 2021, "Ruminating."
*Poetry Society of Vermont—The Mountain Troubadour 75th Anniversary
      Edition 2022*, "First Game of Spring," and "Old Milkweed."
Poetry Society of Vermont—The Mountain Troubadour 2023, "Rain."
Rat's Ass Review, "Muddy Water" October, 2021 (online and print.)
The Lake Poetry Magazine, November 2021 "Lost Words."
The Main Street Rag, Summer 2022 Vol. 27, "Hard Feelings."
Young Raven's Literary Review, December 2021, Issue 15, "Carrying Seeds"
      and "Wooden Fence."
Wilderness House Literary Review, January 2022,"Ghost Apples."
Blue Heron Review, Fall 2022, "Afternoon Nap."
Last Leaves Magazine, April 2022, "Digging Potatoes."
Muddy River Poetry Review, Spring 2022 "Rabbit Rabbit."
Pushing Out the Boat, Scotland, UK, Spring 2023 Issue #17, "Scuttled
      Memories."
PoemCity Anthology, Rootstock Publishing, 2023 pg 155 "Lost Dog."

Publisher: Leah Huete de Maines
Editor: Christen Kincaid
Cover Art: John F. Hogeboom (via Stable Diffusion AI)
Author Photo: Maggie Eaton
Cover Design: Elizabeth R. McCarthy

Order online: www.finishinglinepress.com
            also available on amazon.com

Author inquiries and mail orders:
Finishing Line Press
PO Box 1626
Georgetown, Kentucky 40324
USA

Contents

For my husband, Tim and children, Forrest and Ali.

Lost Words

One day you're living your life like every other day before it
and suddenly it changes
>> and nothing is the same

You run out of words to describe the cup of coffee
>> you are drinking
>> as you sit at the kitchen table, or
maybe,
>> you forget the color of your daughter's hair

Everything is there but not there,
>> and you are living
in the not there but know the there exists without you

Would you have wished you'd known beforehand that this day
would come,
>> or is it just as well you didn't know?

If you'd known maybe you could have flown to Costa Rica
>> walked in lush shade forests where coffee beans grow
>> sipped your coffee there as you listened to the coffee
warbler
>> sing his slow, soft, sweet whistled trill

You could have combed your daughter's hair every night
>> before she went to sleep
>>> and learned the many styles of braids,
>>> one for each school day

She could have had a French braid day, Dutch day,
>> plait day, lace and ladder day

Maybe then when you heard a warbler sing
>> and you held a golden braided rope
>>> you'd always know the words
>>> for a cup of coffee
>>>> and the color of your daughter's hair

the Odd Cat Sanctuary

is where I would like to go
        if the time comes to send me
to a home where scattered minds
           wander in the night

      through old neighborhoods
howling for long lost kittens
         that have grown, moved away

left to sleep all day in sunlit windows
              stretching, rolling between
      dreams of birds and mice

once stalked with grace and power
      wildness ambushing in terror
         leaving death at the door

a gift of unrecognized kindness

Lost in Suburbia

A lone sandhill crane
        awkwardly strolled
through the backyard,

head oscillating,
leggy steps,
halting, hesitant
ready to flee
the moment
life moved.

Lost in a suburban world
where the polygamous robin
        lays her perfect
                blue eggs

and sings her
cheery songs of spring
        above the orderly pink
                and yellow tulips.

While this gangling gray bird
        wanders along
                out of place, missing life
        on the edge
of meadows and wetlands,
        or great open prairies
where she once stretched her wings,
        and danced with abandon
in the wild
with her lifelong love.

Flying Home

Sitting in this winged vessel
        in the sky above
the green and brown
                jigsaw puzzle of earth,

I wonder if birds
        feel the same silent
melancholy when seeing
            their empty nest

        after spring has finished
her blooming, and summer
        turns stale, dropping old
leaves everywhere.

Do they recognize their fledglings
        and see them flourish and fly
            on their own, or have they
lost them somewhere
        in the flight path of time?

I wonder if they pity us
        with our one chance
            to watch our young family
crack open their shells
        and become the beautiful
beings they are meant to be.

For they can fly into spring
        again and again and again
            to soft and downy nestlings,
listen to them squawk, peep,
        and teach them to sing.

Morning Offerings

Hanging laundry outside on the line
on a mid-August morning, listening
to the soundtrack of field crickets

Is a favorite summer chore, though
no chore at all actually, more of
a morning offering to the Sun

As I raise my head and arms up
lifting the wet white sheets
and pinning them in silent prayer

Of thanks for this moment
of quiet meditation that can never
be replaced by a drum rolling dryer

Rain

has left us to wonder—
when will you return
to wash the dust
from our drying bones

as we stand here—withering
barely holding on to curled
paper leaves that rattle
in the faint evening breeze

whispering empty promises
of soft sweet summer showers
and cleansing of souls—yet we
are unforgiven on this parched land

where one day rushing torrents
will come, storming in rage
at our earthly sins—washing away
our gray powdered ashes of guilt

My Dreams

I wish my nightmares
would know they are not
my dreams.

They are the darkest
measure of mankind.
Black storms,

floods where kindness
drowns and floats
like jetsam

discarded from hearts
of once little lambs
now blind,

lost in the nightmare
of untruth and ignorance,
divorced from

a righteous world
where people dream
of love

and peace together,
where understanding
is the sunrise.

Wearing Many Hats

I've always liked wearing hats
a finishing touch on an incomplete painting,
turning an average everyday being
into an interesting character to play

The tin foil space hat I made at five
and wore to our small town library
where the gray haired librarian
smiled and said she liked my hat

At eight, I wore my Dad's sailor hat
as I climbed up the riggings to the crow's nest
high on the roof of our old house
to look for land or whales or enemy ships

In my teens, I found a men's brown fedora
and wore it to a party with dirty bell bottoms,
a clean white blouse embroidered with flowers
as I floated through my hippie days

Then I took a break from being someone,
hatless for years I struggled to find myself
as I wandered, exposed to harsh winds
until my thirties when I stumbled upon

The best of hats in marriage and motherhood,
invisible hats; lace veils, flowery bonnets
that changed with the season, pith helmets,
chef hats, and finally my favorite straw hat

That I wear when my love and I take a stroll
along our country road watching the black-cap
finch flash yellow-gold as he dips and rises
over the beaver marsh and past the falling sun

Songs of Nostalgia

Who teaches newborn leaves
to whisper in the breeze
as they flutter in place
sending soft melodies
aloft to float through spring
accompanied by the sweet scents
of apple blossom and lilac,
singing songs of nostalgia
written long ago
in childhood gardens?

First Game of Spring

Before sugar maples finish
        their sweet drip and welcome
                the warblers, thrushes and finches
        to nest in the crook of a wooden arm

Before old snow slips
        its shady ground
melting in the marsh over the cattail's paw

Before opening day
        when throngs of soaring spectators
                chirp and sing
        at the first pitch of spring

Before dandelion blossoms are cast out
        across bright green fields and pink confetti
                flies from wild stands of crabapple

The peepers and wood frogs
        call out from their watery dugout
        announcing the first game of spring

peeping, quacking and clucking—
        competing for their place
                in the vernal pool of love

Rabbit Rabbit

This morning
in the inky dawn
you whispered
rabbit rabbit
and rolled over
into the comfort
of another
lucky month.

As if life
is a roll
of the dice
and rabbits
run the tables
clearing all bets
just before midnight,
setting a new clock
for those who
believe in destiny
delivered in the night
of each new month.

Daylight Savings

seems like a scam,
selling us daylight
for an hour of sleep

only to take it back
when things get cold
and light is reclaimed

by some dark lord
ruling a tilted world
where the sun burns

down below, until spring
leaps forward into the light
dragging us from bed

as we fall once again
for the man's con—
that time is a real thing

March Light

The heart of winter
        has softened
revealing a golden lamp
        searching for spring.

Its light beam crawls
        across the horizon
                warming February's
white crusty skin.

Casting long shadows
        behind the drooping pine
                that weeps crystal droplets

of joy upon hearing
        the yellow-rumped warbler
sing and flutter,

        calling his love
to join him once again
        as March lights
the way to spring.

Mowing

High up in the wide cast iron seat
        of farmer's tractor, my small frame
                nudged in next to worn denim and sweat,
        giant gnarly tires dragged sharp teeth,
slicing all the meadow flowers, clover
and redtop grasses in our path.

Sitting on the back of an iron monster as it
        spewed black smoke and groaned loudly,
I feared falling, becoming winter fodder
        fed to the lovely lanolin scented sheep.

Now tired and abandoned tractors sit out
        to pasture rusting in place, reminding me
                of their terrifying power and the joy, and fear
        of mowing down summer's sweet life

Muddy Water

I look down into the muddy water
thinking it should be clear, but then,
who am I to judge the world of a frog?

Where they leap and swim from my curious eyes
that hope to see beyond the shallow edge
into the depths of a brown-green pond,

into a world as obscure as the homeless man
who sleeps in the tent across the railroad tracks,
hidden behind the overgrown chokecherry
and poison oak where I see nothing of his life.

Carrying Seeds

Weeds and wildflowers
crackle on cold autumn days
as their dried brittle bones
are snapped underfoot.

Reminding us to step lightly
and look closely at the seeds
with feathers, and all the fallen
beauty returned to the earth.

While tenacious brown burrs
cling tight to life—as we
carry on in rambles
under the steel gray sky.

Old Milkweed

New grasses, wild parsnip,
goldenrod stems, green
            weeds that wake
in wispy breaths
            of morning dew
                        wiping away
night's blank stare
            to see

old milkweed still standing
            there—since last season,
                        rattling death
on the edge of field
            and garden,

brown leathery husks
shriveled and hollow,

relics of seeds with feathers
            that flew with the wind
the day they burst open
            the pod door—escaping

to whorl and dance
in the autumn sun.

Ruminating

Winter is long and dark
in the Kingdom
of cows and poets

where they wait
patiently in their stalls
for signs of spring,

ruminating on dead
red clover—from dried up
fields where honey
bees
danced to the sweet
songs of summer

before Frost's whispering
scythe swung and cut
its deepening swathes

of meadow fodder
for us to reap in time
for the season's end.

Safe Ice

Covering sweet summer
  down below cold waters
Putting spring peepers and
  turtles to their silty mud beds

Steel gray days fade
  to dark freezing nights
North wind sails in to buff
  pond's new clear hard shell

  We safely skate!
Free from the depths
  of our fears, free to fly
    across the mirror glass

Spinning and gliding
  straight lines, half circles
carving scars of joy with
  ice crystal swooshes

Marking our days
  in wool and mittens
On blades we defy gravity
  and winter's frigid hold

Snow Moon

I woke to see your face
covered in moonlight
       quiet light
that crept in through the dark
when we weren't looking.

Seeing Selene in her radiance
       alighting onto you
resting after a long chariot ride
       through time.

You appeared years younger
       in her snow white shadow.

Did she mistake you
       for her Endymion? [En·dym·i·on]

I listened for the crash of waves,
the feel of earth's spin
but heard nothing except
       familiar slow breaths
and felt only the steady warmth
       and softness of our bed.

As you slept on peacefully
       ignoring the celestial intruder
who so rudely interrupted
       my mortal slumber.

Scuttled Memories

We walk away from yesterday
as if it will be there tomorrow
            just as we left it

Like abandoned whaling stations
at the bottom of the world
            table set, kettle waiting

For the return of someone
we once knew, keeping things
            frozen in time

They are stuck in the wooden hull
of memory, where they sit
            and wait unchanged

Until one day a foreigner sails by
wearing their familiar face,
            scuttling you with a smile

Digging Potatoes

Stepping on the edge of this shovel
my full weight sinks down into the dark
cold earth where new potatoes are buried.

Waiting to be lifted into the sunlight,
washed and dried, filled sacks of golden orbs,
treasure that only my ancestors knew

was life itself. The holy host that fed
our people until the blight of man and
nature left them to rot and die—there

in the green fields where old gravestones
now stand—crooked, moss and lichen covered.
Markers of my great long lost aunties,

uncles, cousins who would sit at my table
and laugh at the bounty before them
as I served up my tiny white spuds.

Succession

The tamarack trees that surround
        our house have aged.
Never moving beyond our view
        other than to sway in the wind.

We watched as their needles turned
        golden-yellow before dropping
each autumn, and renewed in spring
        as sage-green, feathery clusters.

Now, only craggy gray trunks
        barely stand, with needleless limbs
cracked and fragile, ready to fall
        in a whisper from the raven's wing.

As gentle a breath that drew our Mémère*
        down the narrow dark staircase
            where she tumbled and fell,
landing hard on the floor below.

Now, we stand in the new open light,
        smell the damp woody earth,
           and watch the raven
fly off, over the distant hills.

*Mémère is a French-Canadian term for grandmother.

Mother's Shadow

I find myself veering off page
to write of solitary nightbirds
       or words that wander along
some winding woods road
       in search of home.

Avoiding her presence,
the dark shadow behind me
       now softly fading
              in early twilight.

Where her beauty and love
       appear as ghosted memories
lost amid the chaos and trauma
       of addiction that followed
              our family through time.

Like the nightbird, I learned
       to adapt and sing in the dark
while waiting for dawn's light
       when love returned
              to a broken heart.

Brother Holy Bird

Since that moment when the Great Blue
      disrupted our graveside mourning,
breaking earth's sullen silence
        with slow swooshing sighs from above,

I see you often at water's edge
      standing still in your gray-blue suit,
the one we, your sisters chose for you
        after your body was flown home.

Clever you—always knowing
      not everyone is destined
to heaven or hell
        nor can we all be angels.

Afternoon Nap

Waking from a nap
under a sunlit window
next to soft fur bodies
sprawled out, asleep.

Dog snoring at my feet,
cat's dreaming claws attached
to the faded blue pillow
that holds my head.

Afraid to move, I lay there
thinking how calm
and zen-like life can be
when your outer being

is held captive by love,
tying you down with threads
so fine the slightest breath
can break loose a room

full of hungry beasts
who at that moment
care nothing of your
personal awakening or
the love that holds you still.

Lost Dog

for Finn

I'm wading through the shock and grief
of finding our dog dead on the floor.

He left us in the night as if he'd
run off, on the track of some wild

creature drawing him deep
into the woods beyond our call.

Lost forever, yet I still call
for him to come home to us

and retrieve the joy he'd left
behind now in shreds, scattered

like all the toys he ever owned.

Hard Feelings

Some
wild apples
hang on
to branches
well past
their season
to fall.

Like grudges,
they hold fast
through cold
winter storms.

Fermenting,
sour little
hearts that
rot in place.

Ghost Apples

The rare
ghost apple,
haunts the
dormant tree
with ice glass
crystal
formed of
freezing rain
wrapping
around the wild
beautiful blush
before death
dissolves its
sweet flesh.

Writings from the Dead

I write as I live my life,
        unfinished and wanting,
yet filled with enduring moments
        that have been stored away

        like the red squirrel in summer, dashing
across our yard, gathering seeds, hiding them
        deep in the cavity of the old rotting tree.

Saving sepia vignettes of a country childhood,
        stashing away wistful images of my children
        blowing dandelion duff across vast green fields,
        standing on a mountaintop on our foggy wedding day.

I wonder, when autumn leaves fall
        and snow buries this world cold,
will my cache be remembered and live on
        or remain in the eternal dark hollow?

Elizabeth McCarthy lives in an old farmhouse in northern Vermont. She began writing poetry during the pandemic when time became a windfall. She self-published her first chapbook *The Old House* in 2020, her poetry manuscript, *Digging Potatoes*, was a finalist for the Hunger Mountain: VCFA May Day Mountain Chapbook Series in 2021. Her chapbook, *Winter Vole* was published by Finishing Line Press in 2022, and in addition to *Hard Feelings*, Finishing Line Press 2024, Elizabeth has an upcoming publication titled, *Wild Silence*, Kelsay Books in 2024. Her poems appear in many literary publications, including; *PoemCity, The Main Street Rag, Young Ravens' Literary Review, Blue Heron Review, ZigZag Literary Magazine, The Lake, The Mountain Troubadour, The Washington Post*. Elizabeth is a member of the Poetry Society of Vermont and an online member of The Lockdown Poets of Aberdeen, Scotland.

When she is not writing, Elizabeth volunteers as the Web Manager and Archivist for the Poetry Society of Vermont. She also spends time running the dirt roads of Vermont with her husband of 35 years, training for Vermont and National Senior Games where they participate in road races and track and field events throughout Vermont and beyond. Elizabeth is also an avid golfer and finds, like writing poetry and running, contentment is fleeting.